# THE CODE THAT WILL ROCK THE PLANET
## AND DESTROY THE RULING CLASS!

# THE
# GAMACODE

## THE FREEING OF THE HUMAN RACE

# TOM KIRKBRIDE

Also by Tom Kirkbride

Gamadin Book Series

Book I - *Gamadin: Word of Honor*
Book II - *Gamadin: Mons*
Book III - *Gamadin: Distant Suns*
Book IV - *Gamadin:* Gazz
Book V - *Gamadin: Core*
Book VI - *Gamadin: The Wild Strain*

*Lakewood,* a Gamadin Prequel

Gamadin Short Stories

*Stinky's Island*
*Surfing Roots*
*Apollos' Flags*
*Incident@Base 5*

Gamadin Titles in the Works

Book VII - *Gamadin: Mamua*

# CopyRight

There are No Copyright restrictions.

Gamacode Rules belong to the Beings of the Planet.

It is their's to copy, quote, post, use, and distribute as they wish.

# Dedication

For the children and the generations of the Future.
Let these rules be your guide.
Let these rules serve you ... always!
Do not dilute them, change them, or tweak them.
For they are your arsenals against servitude!!!

———◆———

A special thank you to
**Carlos Tavares**
(the elephant in the room)
for his contribution to this book,
and his dogged insistence that history
and words have meaning and consequences.

"The Dragon has always believed that the Earth is His,
and of course, he's mistaken."

The Watchman, December 22, 2014

"Human nature, if it changes at all,
changes not much faster than the geological face of the earth."

Alexander Solzhenitsyn

"When people start figuring out that they don't need ruler's,
the world will be completely transformed in a very short time."

Anon

# Gamacode

**PREAMBLE:** The *Gamacode* is law. All Governing Bodies (GB) will obey the *Gamacode*. A Governing Body is any individual (ie. dictator, president, or monarch et al) or group of representatives that has authority over sentient beings.

1. A GB cannot interfere with a being's inherent and inalienable right to have a life free of oppression.
2. A GB cannot interfere with a being's absolute right to arm, protect, and defend one's person, family, community, or property.
3. The GB will be local, accountable, fully open and transparent where the right of public scrutiny shall not be denied.
4. A GB cannot interfere with a being's right to acquire, sell, possess, and to own private property.
5. A GB's duty is to insure a being's right to due process.
6. A GB cannot pass any law forbidding freedom of speech or to congregate "peacefully."
7. A GB cannot suppress a being's right to freedom of worship.
8. A GB cannot create money.
9. A GB cannot establish a central bank.
10. A GB cannot tax or levy a person, property, or business.
11. A GB and its workforce cannot be greater than one, one thousandth percent (.001) of the population they serve.
12. A GB official or representative cannot serve more than one, three-year term in their lifetime.
13. A GB cannot have rights, they have a duty to the beings they represent, and the *Gamacode*.
14. GBs are subject to the laws they pass.
15. A GB cannot have the power to prosecute.
16. A GB cannot create a welfare state.
17. A GB cannot issue debt or operate in a deficit.
18. A GB cannot own land.
19. A GB cannot create a secret, clandestine organization, or military force.
20. A GB cannot revoke the *Gamacode*.
21. What the Gamacode does not cover is left to the GB of the particular society, country, or state they represent, to run as they choose, as long as the *Gamacode* is not violated.

**CONCLUSION:** The *Gamacode* is absolute and unequivocal. The *Gamacode* does not require trust or acceptance. No entity, being, or Governing Body is exempt. The *Gamacode* is not amendable. The *Gamacode* is not living, transitional, or temporary document or set of rules. The *Gamacode* is enduring and forever. Governing Bodies and/or Individuals violating the *Gamacode* will be immediately excommunicated to a world other than their own with no recourse of return.

# Introduction

The *Gamacode* is an apolitical, non-religious, unalterable plan to free the beings of our planet. The Code may sound crazy, laughable, or even a fantasized dream to many, especially to those in power. But that doesn't make the *Gamacode* wrong or impossible to achieve. It is a body of rules the beings of the planet must achieve or the planet will not survive. It is as simple as that.

The governing bodies (GB) of the planet will NEVER give up their power willingly. They will use by whatever means to increase their rule just as every GB has done throughout history. In some cases the GB will become so powerful they will make themselves presidents or dictators for life. Critics will say the idea of a president-for-life is nonsense, saying that could never happen. Yet, recently China has approved the removal of the two-term limit on its president, effectively allowing Xi Jinping to remain in power for life. **(https://www.bbc.com/news/world-asia-china-43361276)**

But that's China, you say. Unlike the United States, China is a Communist dictatorship. Our Constitution protects us. The XXII Amendment limits our president to two, four-years terms. Since the turn of the last century the Constitution has steadily been eroded, and our freedoms have been taken from us little by little by those who believe, for their own selfish reasons, it is a "living document" that should be subject to change according to the times. Justice Scalia once said, "Of course it's just words on paper, what our framers would have called a 'parchment guarantee'."

"Here's the thing: We already have a president for life. Sure, the names, faces, and parties have changed over the years, but really, when you drill down under the personalities and political theater, you'll find that the changing names and faces are merely cosmetic no matter who sits on the throne. The office of the president of the United States has, for all intents and purposes, become a unilateral power unto itself."

". . . in recent years, American presidents (Trump, Obama, the Bushes, Clinton, etc.) have claimed the power to completely and almost unilaterally alter the landscape of this country for good or for ill.

The powers amassed by each successive president through the negligence of Congress and the courts—powers which add up to a toolbox of terror for an imperial ruler—empower whomever occupies the Oval Office to act as a dictator, above the law and beyond any real accountability.

So are you willing to bet your children's future that without a major directional change in the power of our government that a President for Life cannot happen here in the United States?

"As I make clear in my book," writes John Whitehead via the Rutherford Institute, "*Battlefield America: The War on the American People*, the only thing that will save us now is a concerted, collective commitment to the U.S. Constitution's principles of limited government, a system of checks and balances, and a recognition that they—the president, Congress, the courts, the military, the police, the technocrats and plutocrats and bureaucrats—answer to and are accountable to "we the people."

However, Mr. Whitehead is mistaken in the sense that the phrase "We the People" are oppressive words often used to add a rightful sound to a democratic society, run by the people. It is not the *Gamacode's* intent to give power to the masses. To a being, yes, but not to the masses. Throughout history, democracies, like all forms of socialism, have always failed. ALWAYS! Democracies fail because they are designed to impose majority rule at the expense of the minority. It is human nature to protect ones power. Majority rule always, ALWAYS morphs into mob rule. Thus, a democracy suddenly becomes a GB and fails to protect the rights of beings in the minority. The *Gamacode* will protect all beings whether they are the majority or the minority.

Socialism fails as it always, ALWAYS has throughout history in a different manner because it eliminates what Adam Smith referred to as the "invisible hand" of markets and the destruction of private property rights. Under socialism or communism, call it what you want, beings do not own anything . . . the State does, thus violating the first and fourth rules of the *Gamacode*:

The limits on governments should not be restricted to just one country or nation, either. The limits must be world-wide! In order for the totality of the human race to survive a global event such as nuclear war, an extraterrestrial meteor strike not unlike those that have happened several times in the past (dinosaurs' extinction, Younger Dryas event), the coming ice age, or an alien visitation, we must change how we see our GBs. We must change our perception of them on a global scale. The *Gamacode* does not purpose to control a being, or go against human nature. The Code was created to do one thing: drastically reduce or eliminate all forms of GBs, including all-powerful monarchs, dictators, and institutions such as corporations, banks, or religious institutions by downsizing them to the point where their GBs will become a small fraction of their previous size or wither away and die a lonely death. The Code believes that one day beings will wonder why they ever put up with unaccountable, irresponsible, elitist GBs for so long. Across the globe, our freedoms, our liberty, our humanity, and our hard earned sweat are stolen from us every day. Don't believe it? Try neglecting to pay your income tax or property tax, and see how long it takes a GB to come to your door to confiscate your property and bank accounts by force without due process. Throughout history, that has always been the case. GBs are ruthless. "They don't play nice, by any means." (Jeff Berwick) Unless by force or revolution, they have never returned power to the beings of the community, but GBs have always taken it!

It is also a fact that governments have killed more of their own people than all the wars in recorded history combined!

The solution against this loss of freedom and mass extinction is found in the *Gamacode*. The Code will save life on the planet from total annihilation. For the first time in our planetary history, the power of ALL GOVERNING BODIES everywhere will be crushed or drastically reduced forever.

Rest assured, the governing elite will never give up their power willingly. They will instill fear in the world's population, telling the beings of the planet there will be global chaos, countries destroyed, and millions of lives lost. The very thought of a being having responsibility for oneself and for each other is terrifying to a great number of people. After all, the slave mentally that only governments, institutions, religious bodies, and monarchies can lead us, take care of us, keep the peace, and give us happiness has been cultivated in us for eons. That is so untrue. The beings of the planet are billions strong against thousands of GBs. We can do it. The beings of the planet can change our world forever for the better. The politicians and so-called leaders won't do it for us. That would mean giving up their own power and control.

*"The whole aim of practical politics"*, wrote HL Mencken, *"is to keep the populace alarmed (and hence clamorous to be led to safety) by menacing it with an endless series of hobgoblins, most of them imaginary."*

Freedom is not a dream. It can and will be a reality. It has been proven over and over again throughout history, where populations are allowed to flourish and exercise their own freewill, the greatest advances in science, medicine, math, art and literature have occurred. A free and inventive mind knows no limits. We can stop the killing, the wasteful destruction of our resources, and stop all wars by eliminating the root cause of it all . . . GOVERNING BODIES and their co-conspirators: the banks and various media, and religious outlets! That fact is the elephant in the room . . . ALWAYS!

Governing bodies are no different than the Mafia. They are the shelter for corruption. Rome didn't create an empire by having meetings. They did it with their massive army killing all those who opposed them.

The *Gamacode* will destroy this slave mentally overnight. As you read through the Code, ask yourself which rule would you eliminate to achieve freedom for the beings of our world? If the United States didn't have an IRS with its enforcers backing it up, would the GB be able to rob the American people of their economic freedom? Could Stalin, Pol Pot, or Mao have slaughtered tens of millions of their own people without their vast armies? Would Britain have conquered over half the globe without its navy? Would America's debt have amounted to over a quadrillion with a small government the size of the one stated in Rule 11 of the *Gamacode*? Or do you believe a GB creates a welfare system, health care subsidies, and free government schools out of the goodness of their heart? The answer, of course, is no to all these questions. They should not and will not control the human race.

"They want to turn us into bots. Some of us are already bots. Some of us were born to parents that are bots. The only thing that will keep you free is to challenge your own mental bias. Think while it's still legal!" *Anon.*

Is it any different than when Roman emperors tossed bread to the masses in the Coliseum? I don't think so . . .

The *Gamacode* is the door to planetary freedom for us all!

*T.K.*

# What is the Gamacode?

THE *GAMACODE* IS a set of strict rules that all Governing Bodies (GB) on the planet Earth must obey or this planet of beings will not survive. They are twenty-one laws that politicians, monarchs, religious bodies, public officials, and despots must follow or they will suffer sudden and severe consequences. Make this very clear, the *Gamacode* does not control the sentient beings of the planet. The Code is strictly concerned with the GBs planet-wide. For they, along with their co-conspirators the banks, are responsible for stripping the beings of the planet of their freedom through countless wars, mass genocide, and democide. They are the thieves of our freedom, our liberty, and our pursuit of private property for all of mankind's history.

Lord Acton said it best: "Power tends to corrupt, and absolute power corrupts absolutely. Great men are almost always bad men . . ."

Throughout our past, corrupt GBs have become so powerful

and crooked that life for the beings subjugated by this ruling class has become unbearable, oppressive, and deadly. This is hardly a new concept. Brave men and women have been fighting against oppression and slavery by GBs throughout history all the way up to the present day where the "yellow vests" in France are now revolting against their GB. Frederick Douglas, William Wallace, Joan of Arc, Gandi, Spartacus, Alexander Solzhenitsyn, Ayn Rand and Julian Assange are just a few who come to mind who have led this fight for Freedom. Can one imagine what Galileo might have accomplished if the Catholic Church, in February, 1616, had not declared in its Inquisitorial commission that his writings were "foolish and absurd in philosophy" because it explicitly contradicted the Holy Scripture? GBs have stifled the intellectual growth, inventive spirit, and freedom of our great and beautiful planet during the entire time of their existence. To meet the needs of the planet's future, which will one day include joining the community of planets in our galaxy, and who knows, maybe beyond our galaxy, freedom, liberty, and self-determination of the individual must be allowed to grow and flourish freely without interruption or suppression.

The *Gamacode* has no political objective other than to see the freedom of the individual prevail. Today, there are many whose lives and incomes depend on the GB never solving the freedom issue. They exist as so-call rebels against tyranny, but in reality they are frauds, for their total existence and livelihoods depend on the continued oppression of the people they are supposed to represent.

The *Gamacode* rules are impartial and separate from any ideology, belief, or the color of one's skin. It is linked to no individual, group, crusade, or country. The *Gamacode* crosses all borders. It is everywhere GBs exist on the planet. It is not a living Code, either, nor can it be changed, amended, or altered. Have the rules of Chess changed in over a thousand years? The Code is, must be, and will be the universal LAW for Governing Bodies planet-wide!

"People should not be afraid of their governments. Governments should be afraid of their people." Anon.

The *Gamacode* does not seek to make a Utopian society, or a one-world government, or to destroy one's culture for the benefit of the Code. It does not eliminate governments, either. What it does do is limit the size and scope of GBs drastically by laying out a GB's duties toward the beings of our planet. The *Gamacode* will not stop individuals from committing crime or being unkind to each other. It is a fallacy to believe human nature can be altered by any code or body of rules. Not even the Ten Commandments has stopped killing or theft or adultery. The *Gamacode* understands this, and does not pretend to fix or solve man's weaknesses or moral shortcomings. Communities will be responsible for their own citizen's misconduct, contracts, fraud, and the rights of individuals. Leaders of communities, however, will be held accountable if they break the rules of the *Gamacode*. Societies' citizens will be well armed and offer protection for their own communities. What the *Gamacode* will do is stop the out-of-control power grab of GBs that has led to out of control wars, massive killings by uncontrolled militaries, secret organizations, and/or the wholesale murder and slavery by various methods of mind control of beings.

"The urge to save humanity is almost always a false front for the urge to rule!" H.L. Menchn

Governing Bodies are by their very nature selfish and are run by, let's call them what they are, Gangs! They are the instigators of mass destruction, all wars, and corporate corruption. GBs are the shelter of corruption, i.e. banks, churches, military industrial complexes, politicians, voter fraud, back door alliances, lies, secret organizations, and on into infinity. The GBs become so big and so powerful they have no obligation or responsibility to serve the beings they represent. Often, there are no consequences for bad GB leadership or the passing of self-serving laws. GBs are often immune, like politicians, to prosecution and suffer little or no penalties for foolish decisions. Once large sums of money, expensive homes, and their kingly toys no longer serve these governing elites, once they have matured, they want to play god. These so called leaders and their egos believe they alone have the power to shape the world and are above the law. When GBs are cut to the bare minimum, together with their loss of military might, and the forfeiture of their taxing power, their system of tyranny will collapse and fade away. Freedom will prevail. The State and its political hacks will no longer exist as a force feared by the beings of the planet.

The *Gamacode*, once applied, will have the power to transform the planet into a free and peaceful environment, adding deep richness to everyone's existence, not just for a chosen few. Imagine a life without threat of senseless regulations, losing one's property over taxes, of trumped up asset forfeitures, endless levies to pay for pointless wars, militaries, and government and corporate corruption.

For the first time in world history the *Gamacode* will make true private property ownership possible!

Freedom is the life-blood of a growing and prosperous world at all levels. When the citizens discover that no politicians, House of Commons, Parliaments, Congress, Prime Ministers, Presidents, Kings and Queens are required to rule over them, the world will be transformed in a positive way. Freedom will become the norm. The freed beings of the planet will never go back. Control of the population is the lifeblood of the GB. The loss of authority will be their doom!

Without true freedom there is no liberty. Freedom and an all-powerful, unchecked GB cannot coexist. Entire civilizations die because the GB sucks the lifeblood from their producers to the point they no longer are able to harvest, produce, or create anything. "No civilization has ever outlived its food supply . . . EVER!"

Today, the *U.S. Constitution* has been completely nullified. Government agents and their enforcers can do whatever they desire with impunity. The reality is beings do not have rights. We are no longer citizens of the state, we are its subjects. We exist by government's largess. It is the burden of individuals to prove otherwise. In today's world rights exist only if one has the money to hire expensive lawyers who price themselves far too high, which ensures people are not defended. That has been the way throughout history and will continue without exception, unless the *Gamacode* is LAW!

"There is no government anywhere; you are all absolutely free. There is no restraint that cannot be escaped. We are all absolutely free. If everybody could go into meditation at will, nobody could be controlled — by fear of prison, by fear of whips or electroshock, by fear of death, even. All existing society is based on keeping those fears alive, to control the masses. Ten people who know would be more dangerous than a million armed anarchists."

Robert Anton Wilson *Cat Trilogy* (1979)

"We hold these truths to be self-evident, that all men are created equal, that they are endowed by their Creator with certain unalienable Rights, that among these are Life, Liberty and the pursuit of ~~Happiness~~ private property."

*The Declaration of Independence, July 4, 1776*--edited

# Rule One

*"A Governing Body cannot interfere with a being's fundamental and undeniable right to enjoy a life free of oppression."*

Ultimately, a government's soul purpose is to control the lives of beings they represent for what they say is the "greater good" of the community. The beings of the planet have been programmed to believe a GB is the unbiased arbiter of the community's affairs. However, history has shown time and again, like a broken record, the exact opposite is true. GBs are often the source of corruption, destruction, and lawlessness for the simple reason there are no consequences for their corrupt activities. Like a festering wound, the GB's uncontrolled growth is the refuge of dishonesty, fraud, deceitful central banks, corporations, politicians, and secret government organizations.

Absorbed in its own self-importance to maintain their power and to make themselves relevant, GBs must control all aspects of people's lives. As time goes by and opposition arises against the GB, more restrictions are imposed upon the community, more laws are passed which in turn lead to bigger and more lethal means of control in the name of the greater good. The GB then imprisons the rebels against the state, crushing them with loss of freedom, or in the worse case scenario, deadly force. Wounded Knee, Branch Dravidians, Ruby Ridge, Dresden, Yokohama, Hiroshima, the Holocaust, William Wallace, the Mayans, Spanish Inquisition, Pol-Pot, and on and on through history show how the GB eradicates its opposition. GBs will continue to massacre the beings of the planet until their rule once and for all . . . ENDS!

As the *Gamacode* is being written, there is a movement taking place in France that is a perfect example of when a GB becomes too large and controlling citizens must rise up and fight for their freedom. It is commonly called the *gilets jaunes* or "yellow vests" protests. This crusade, led by everyday individuals who just want to live their lives in peace without oppression, has caught the ruling elites off guard. It began when the GB raised taxes on an already overtaxed state. The yellow vests have become a rallying point against the GB of France. The movement has caught on across the globe to the point where paranoid and weak GBs have forbidden the wearing of yellow vests.

"Beings are systematically manipulated into seeing ourselves as totally different and at odds with one another, but the truth of the matter is virtually all of us currently living on this beautiful planet share something very significant in common with one another. We all reside in countries run by and for the benefit of a tiny group of lawless and unscrupulous people. While some nations are clearly in far worse shape than others, we all live in very corrupt and increasingly unfree societies.

Because humans are easily divided and conquered, both within our own countries and on a global level, the few are able to easily rule over the many. If we can somehow find a way to resist power elite manipulations and unite to focus our attention on the true root of our problems, there's nothing we can't accomplish."

Ref: "Can Yellow Vests Protests Go Global?" Michael Krieger: https://libertyblitzkrieg.com/2018/12/11/can-the-yellow-vests-protests-go-global/

Today, the French people are leading the way, and it is an important lesson for us all to see: Beings of the planet can fight back. They can restore freedom; for they must if humanity is to survive.

The *Gamacode*, once implemented, is the path to freedom for all beings of the planet, not just a select few.

"First rule of any tyrannical Governing Body is to disarm the population before seizing power and killing them."

Mike Dennis

"Guns are our friends because in a country without guns, I'm what's known as "prey." All females are."

Ann Coulter

"The rifle itself has no moral stature, since it has no will of its own. Naturally, it may be used by evil men for evil purposes, but there are more good men than evil, and while the latter cannot be persuaded to the path of righteousness by propaganda, they can certainly be corrected by good men with rifles."

Jeff Cooper, Art of the Rifle

If those states which did not have right-to-carry concealed gun provisions had adopted them in 1992, approximately 1,570 murders; 4,177 rapes; and over 60,000 aggravate assaults would have been avoided yearly.

John R. Lott Jr.

# Rule Two

"A Governing Body cannot interfere with a being's absolute right to arm, protect, and defend one's person, family, community, or property."

The New World colonies of the Americas understood this rule and made it the 2nd Amendment to the *U.S. Constitution*. It was not the last amendment, or the sixth, it was the second in line of importance to the Bill of Rights.

*"A well regulated militia being necessary to the security of a free State, the right of the people to keep and bear arms shall not be infringed."*

The right of a person to protect one's self, family, community, or property is fundamental. No GB has the power to disarm an individual of their right to defend themselves by whatever means necessary. GBs view an armed citizen as a threat to their power. Cities like Chicago, Baltimore, Paris, London, Caracas, St. Louis, Los Angeles, and New York (and there are many more) are out of control with crime and daily killings. In all these places a citizen's right to carry a weapon to protect themselves is severely restricted or forbidden by laws against gun ownership. In communities where gun laws have little or no restrictions, peace thrives. A now famous 'gun rights' city of Kennesaw, Georgia, passed a law requiring gun ownership in every household. Crime dropped by 89% in the first year. Kennesaw is not unique. It has been proven time and again that when citizens are engaged, and given the responsibility of defending themselves, the community as a whole is safer every time it is tried. Furthermore, it is not up to the GB to decide what is the right or wrong way to defend one's self, property, and community. The question is not whether a 10-round magazine clip is too big or too little or whether a so-called assault rifle is forbidden just by the way it looks and shoots, or is more deadly than a "normal" hunting rifle. Yet, a GB can possess an atomic device that will kill millions in an instant. What kind of logic is that? As long as the citizenry is accountable for their actions, and weapons are not used in an offensive manner or in a lawless way, the right of individuals to own weapons of their choice shall not be questioned or interfered with by any GB.

Finally, one last thought to keep in mind. Many progressives say the U.S. ranks 3rd in the world in murders by guns. But if you remove the cities of Chicago, Detroit, Washington D.C., St. Louis, and New Orleans, the U.S. then ranks 189th out of 193 countries in the world! Additionally, all five cities listed above have STRICT gun laws passed by progressive Democrats who have been in office for decades.

Bottomline: More guns, less crime. The framers of the *U.S. Constitution* knew this and this is why they made the right to have a gun number two in the *Bill of Rights*.

The administration of government, like guardianship ought to be directed to the good of those who confer, not of those who receive the trust.

Marcus Tullius Cicero

# Rule Three

*"A Governing Body will be local, accountable, fully open, and transparent where the right of public scrutiny shall not be denied."*

NO SECRETS! Trust of the community is the primary duty of all GBs. To this end, the GB and its representatives in all cases are responsible for their actions. The GB will at all times maintain an "open book" policy toward public inspection, meetings, and decisions. Closed-door gatherings, secret arrangements, and/or undisclosed compacts or alliances are forbidden and will violate the *Gamacode*. Those that violate the community trust will be immediately subject to a public or oversight hearing. Depending on the severity of the infraction, they will be suspended or relieved of their GB duties or sentenced to an off-world facility. There is nothing the GB does, discusses, or votes on that is not open to public scrutiny by the community.

If history could teach us anything, it would be that private property is inextricably linked with civilization.

Ludwig von Mises

Nobody spends somebody else's money as carefully as he spends his own. Nobody uses somebody else's resources as carefully as he uses his own. So if you want efficiency and effectiveness, if you want knowledge to be properly utilized, you have to do it through the means of private property.

Milton Friedman

# Rule Four

A GB cannot interfere with a being's right to acquire, sell, possess, and enjoy private property."

Individual property rights are the hallmark of a free and open society. It is an individual's solemn right to use, sell, or enjoy their legally acquired property as they see fit so long as there is no harm to others or to the community. It is no concern of the GB what property owners do with their property. However, a property owner cannot, for example, pour sewage in a river that will harm others downstream. If a property owner wishes to create a lake on his property, it is his right to do so as long as no harm has come to others or the right of other property owners to enjoy their property is not violated.

Property forfeiture laws are also prohibited under Rule #4 of the Code.

"Every day, IRS agents levy liens on homes, bank accounts, and businesses; they confiscate cars, furniture, boats, and other personal property without the constitutional protections of due notice, hearing, and due process. If a person forcibly resists, government agents kill him for resisting arrest."

Jacob G. Hornberger

The civil forfeiture law - if something so devoid of due process can be dignified as law - is an incentive for perverse behavior: Predatory government agencies get to pocket the proceeds from property they seize from Americans without even charging them with, let alone convicting them of, crimes. Criminals are treated better than this because they lose the fruits of their criminality only after being convicted.

George Will

# Rule Five

## "A GB's duty is to insure a being's right to due process."

A GB will protect and respect all legal rights of an individual as to insure no random loss of life, liberty, or property by the GB outside the law has taken place. The idea of "due process" is a concept that dates back as far as the *Magna Carta*: "No man of what state or condition he be, shall be put out of his lands or tenements nor taken, nor disinherited, nor put to death, without he be brought to answer by due process of law." The responsibility of insuring the rights of individuals lies with the GB representatives and their agents, delegates, or deputies. GB representatives can and will be individually accountable for an accuses right to due process. GBs cannot hide behind a protective wall of immunity simply because they are representatives of the GB.

If the freedom of speech is taken away, then dumb and silent we may be led, like sheep to the slaughter.

George Washington

# Rule Six

"A GB cannot pass any law forbidding freedom of speech or to congregate "peacefully.""

Freedom to speak one's mind and to assemble peacefully are the backbone of an individual's liberty and shall not be denied by the GB. The key word here is "peacefully." As stated in law over the centuries, a person does not have the right to yell fire in a crowded theatre, or speak in such a way as to cause harm to another individual, or congregate for illegitimate, criminal, or unlawful purposes.

As of late, the once bastion of freedom of speech, colleges and universities of America have turned against opposing speech. Open debate is ridiculed. No longer is it acceptable to voice an opposing opinion without be verbally abused and in many cases, physically harmed for having an opposing opinion. In a free society, one must have the ability to openly and peacefully discuss the abuse of power of our government and the violations of our Bill of Rights. A peaceful free market of ideas must prevail and must not be silenced because it may hurt one's feelings.

"America is a land rooted in the ideas of a free society: the freedom to be who you are, to speak your mind and to innovate. By silencing our students and young people, we have started down a slippery slope. It is up to us to fight back to ensure that our First Amendment rights remain protected—not just on college campuses, but everywhere in America." Time Magazine: by Cliff Maloney, jr., October 13, 2016

"Religion is like a pair of shoes.....Find one that fits for you, but don't make me wear your shoes."

George Carlin

# Rule Seven

"A GB cannot suppress a being's right to freedom of worship."

A beings right to worship is fundamental. Forcing others to worship is forbidden. Freedom of religion is a principle that supports the freedom of an individual or community, in public or private, to manifest religion or belief in teaching, practice, worship, and observance. This would include the right to change one's religion or beliefs without punishment or persecution for one's beliefs. In a country where there is a state religion, GBs must not interfere and must permit a person's right to worship as they so choose without intimidation, harassment, or oppression. Under the Gamacode the right to believe what a person, group, or religion wishes cannot be suppressed as long as that religion allows the right to practice openly and outwardly in a public manner but does not interfere with the freedom and pursuit of happiness of the community.

Gold is money and everything else is credit.

J.P. Morgan

"If you put the federal government in charge of the Sahara Desert, in five years there'd be a shortage of sand."

Milton Friedman

Giving money and power to government is like giving whiskey and car keys to teenage boys.

P.J. O'Rourke

Tulips are not durable, not scarce, not programmable, not fungible, not verifiable, not divisible, and hard to transfer. But tell me more about your analogy...

Naval

# Rule Eight

## "A Governing Body cannot create money."

Throughout history GBs have used money as a system of control. It is their ultimate power behind the throne. There is a famous Rothchild banker quote that states: "Give me control of a nation's money and I care not who makes it's laws." Whether a Rothchild said this is questionable. However, the statement is profound, regardless of who said it.

"Since gold is honest money, it is hated by the dishonest man."

Bitcoin is a real asset, minted from energy, the fundamental commodity of the universe. Fernando Nieto

The real story is that bankster dishonesty is making the World yearn for honest money – i.e. gold/silver/Bitcoin.

Money is a medium of exchange. In the islands of the South Pacific, seashells were once used to purchase fruit and animals. Cattle, bales of hay, and of course, gold and silver are also forms of money. As far back as the Roman GB the value of a silver dinar became less and less when the GB began substituting cheaper metals for the silver until the once 100% silver dinar became less than 10% silver. This was done so the GB could retain their power by controlling the money supply.

Today, nearly all money has little or no precious metal behind it and has been substituted with worthless paper. It is not "real" money. The practice of creating money out of nothing has led to so much abuse by the GBs across the planet that citizens' accounts and life savings are being robbed daily by the lost valve of their currency. Whether it be rubles, pounds, francs, yen, renminbi, or the world's reserve currency, the dollar, they are all losing value. In 1913, the U.S. dollar was once worth 1.00. Today, over a hundred years later, that same dollar is worth less than a nickel because the GB and its surrogate, the Federal Reserve Bank, a private institution, has destroyed the value of the money by printing too much paper money with no value behind it. The GB has stolen it as much as any thief. All money must have value that cannot be created out of nothing. Like gold, silver, even digital currency such as Bitcoin, there must be precise value created by nature. Why is a digital Bitcoin like gold or silver? It is not backed by anything. It's made up of only 1's and 0's? Bitcoin itself may not have substance but it is a real asset because it is created by energy, the fundamental commodity of the universe. Once this is fully understood by the citizenry, gold's market value will skyrocket. There will no force on Earth that will stop this reset from happening. For this thievery to stop, the responsibility of value must be left to an unbiased, blind market that will be the final arbiter of worth. Gold, silver, and a decentralized digital currency such as Bitcoin is the only money worth considering.

Gold, silver, or its digital equal is the ultimate protection from theft by GB currency debasement.

"You are a den of vipers and thieves. I intend to rout you out, and by the eternal God, I will rout you out!"

> Andrew Jackson, 7th President of the United States

"Money has no motherland; financiers are without patriotism and without decency; their sole object is gain."

> Napoleon Bonaparte

"...central banks cannot really manage anything. They must pretend to be in control, but are simply sitting in the back seat of a taxi with a kangaroo driving."

> Posted Jan 14, 2019 by Martin Armstrong

The "Fed" is NOT the Bank of the United States. It is not part of the government... it's privately owned by guess who? The banks!"

> Anon

# Rule Nine

## "A GB cannot establish a central bank."

Central banks have been created, first and foremost, to fill governments' coffers. This is to increase the kings' or elected governments' financial means through an inflationary scheme – usually too elaborate and too treacherous for most people to see through. Central banks are instrumental for putting the ruler — or the ruling class — into a position where they can plunder the people on a grand scale, and by way of redistributing the loot, making a growing number of people financially and socially dependent on them.

To that end, central banks have been assigned the monopoly of money production. This has made it possible to replace commodities or "natural money" with unbacked paper or fiat money. Central banks provide commercial banks with unbacked money, and then commercial banks are free to pyramid a multiple of fiat commercial bank money on top of it.

The following is an article by Michael Snyder that explains the dangers of a central bank in a very clear and understanding way.

"Central banking has truly taken over the entire planet. At this point, the only major nation on the globe that docs not have a central bank is North Korea. Yes, there are some small island countries that do not have a central bank, but even so, more than 99.9% of the population of the world still lives in a country that has a central bank.

So how has this happened? How have we gotten the entire planet to agree that central banking is the best system? Did the people of the world willingly choose this? Of course not. There has never been a single vote where the people of a nation have willingly chosen to establish a central bank. Instead, what has happened is that central banks have been imposed on all of us.

All over the world, people have been told that monetary issues are "too important" to be subject to politics, and that the only solution is to have a group of unelected, unaccountable bankers control those things for us."

So what is a central bank? As defined by Wikipedia a central bank, reserve bank, or monetary authority is an institution that manages a state's currency, money supply, and interest rates. Central banks also usually oversee the commercial banking system of their respective countries.

In the United States, we are told that we have a free market system. But in a true free market system, market forces would determine what interest rates are. We wouldn't need anyone to "set interest rates" for us.

"And why have we given a private banking cartel (the Federal Reserve) the authority to create and manage our money supply? The *U.S. Constitution* specifically delegates that authority to Congress.
It is not as if we actually need the Federal Reserve. In fact, the greatest period of economic growth in U.S. history happened during the decades before the Federal Reserve was created.

Unfortunately, a little over 100 years ago our leaders decided that it would be best to turn over our financial future to a newly created private banking cartel that was designed by very powerful Wall Street interests. Since that time, the value of our currency has diminished by more than 96 percent and our national debt has become more than 5000 times larger!

But despite all of the problems, the vast majority of Democrats and the vast majority of Republicans are not even willing to consider slightly curtailing the immense power of the Federal Reserve. And the idea of getting rid of the Fed altogether is tantamount to blasphemy to most of our politicians.

Of course, the same thing is true all over the planet. Central banks are truly "the untouchables" of the modern world. Even though everybody can see what they are doing, to date there has not been a single successful political movement anywhere on the globe to shut a central bank down. Instead, in recent years we have seen the reach of central banking just continue to expand.

Central banks are specifically designed to trap nations in debt spirals from which they can never possibly escape. Today, the debt to GDP ratio for the entire planet is up to an all-time high record of 286 percent. Humanity is being enslaved by a perpetual debt machine, but most people are not even aware that it is happening.

It is time for an awakening. We need to educate as many people as possible about why we need to get rid of the central banks. The global elite dominate us because we allow them to dominate us. Their debt-based system greatly enriches them while it enslaves the remainder of the planet. We need to expose their evil system and the dark agenda behind it while we still have time.

Zerohedge.com : Guess How Many Nations In The World Do Not Have A Central Bank? 06/10/2015 Submitted by Michael Snyder via The Economic Collapse blog,

"I'm not against people who have money, who like money, who go crazy for money," Mujica said. "But in politics we have to separate them. We have to run people who love money too much out of politics, they're a danger in politics... People who love money should dedicate themselves to industry, to commerce, to multiply wealth. But politics is the struggle for the happiness of all." Uruguayan President Jose Mujica

Further Reading and video
--G. Edward Griffin:  The Creature from Jekyll Island: A Lecture on the Federal Reserve
--Exposing the Federal Reserve by Glen Beck:  Youtube video: https://youtu.be/vB5LK-jihgk
--Michael Snyder: 100 Reasons to Shutdown the Federal Reserve: http://theeconomiccollapseblog.com/archives/on-the-100th-anniversary-of-the-federal-reserve-here-are-100-reasons-to-shut-it-down-forever

"Taxes were not raised to carry on wars, wars were raised to carry on taxes."

Thomas Paine

Taxes are the price you pay for living in a civilized society.

WRONG!

"Taxes are the price you pay so you won't
get kidnapped by the government!"

George Carlin

"I have never understood why it is "greed" to want to keep the money you have earned but not greed to want to take someone else's money."

Thomas Sowell

# Rule Ten

"A Governing Body cannot tax or levy a person, property, or business."

In a free society, wealth is obtained by inheritance, or by one's sweat, energy, knowledge or skill, or when a someone sticks a gun in your face and says: "Give me your money or else." In the United States and most countries around the world, the latter is the preferred method of thievery.

Andrew Napolitano via the Mises Institute states: "With a tax code that exceeds 72,000 pages in length and consumes more than six billion person hours per year to determine taxpayers' taxable income, with an IRS that has become a feared law unto itself, and with a government that continues to extract more wealth from every taxpaying American every year, is it any wonder that April 15th is a day of dread in America?

This mafia-like thievery is planet-wide for the simple reason it is human nature for GBs to control others by force. This force comes through the control over an individual's money and property. As much as the GB would like us to believe, taxing is not voluntary. It is a forced payment. Stop paying your taxes and watch how fast your property or freedom is taken from you without due process.

How would our government run without taxes, one asks? Simple. For the first 150 years of America's existence the federal government was run by user fees and sales of government land and assessments to the states for services rendered. It rejected the Hamiltonian view that the feds could take whatever they wanted, and it followed the Jeffersonian first principle that the only moral commercial exchanges are those that are fully voluntary.

This worked well until the progressives took over the government in the first decade of the 20th century. They persuaded enough Americans through propaganda that only the "rich" would be taxed so their state legislatures would ratify the Sixteenth Amendment during the dead of night when , which gave the government to tax income. It was designed to tax the rich and redistribute wealth. They promised the American public that the income tax would never exceed 3 percent of income and would only apply to the top 3 percent of earners. How wrong – or deceptive – they were. Today, Tax Freedom Day is the day the average American earns enough money to pay off their total tax obligations for the year. If one lives in New York for example, that day is May 14th, but if you live in Louisiana, it is April 5th. In other words, at the very least one has to work over a third of the year for the government before they can begin working for themselves. According to the government, it is presumed that we don't really own our property. It accepts the Marxist notion that the state owns everything, even when we die. Beings are only permitted to keep and use whatever the states deems it will allow us to keep so we won't riot in the streets. And then it steals and uses whatever it can politically get away with. Contribution by Tyler Durden  Mon, 04/17/2017 – Zerohedge. com

This is not how our country began, "Setting forth his renowned dictum that the power to tax involves the power to destroy," Chief Justice John Marshall declared that the states (and, by inference, local governments) "have no power, by taxation or otherwise, to retard, impede, burden or in any manner control the operations of the constitutional laws enacted by Congress."

With the advent of Rule 11 (the severe reduction of the government workforce), Rule 16 (outlawing of welfare states), and Rule 19 (the elimination of military forces and secret organizations) along with other reduction rules within the *Gamacode*, such revenue producing schemes will be a thing of the past. The *Gamacode* will end the practice of taxation against humanity forever and return freedom to the beings of the planet who will have the right to keep the wealth and property they earn without fear of losing it by GB theft.

A government big enough to give you everything you want is a government big enough to take from you everything you have.

Gerald R. Ford

"No government ever voluntarily reduces itself in size. Government programs, once launched, never disappear. Actually, a government bureau is the nearest thing to eternal life we'll ever see on this earth!"

Ronald Reagan

"As government expands, liberty contracts."

Ronald Reagan

# Rule Eleven

"A Governing Body and its workforce and representatives cannot be greater than one, one thousandth percent (.001) of the population.

In its truest, most basic form, a limited government is a body whose main function is the protection of people and their property, and it levies just enough duties to finance services related to these purposes, such as courts, public projects, and law enforcement. Otherwise, it stays out of people's and businesses' affairs. It is not the government's job to tell anyone what they must earn per hour, what amount of school they must acquire, or how one must invest their retirement funds, or how many miles per gallon a vehicle should attain before it can be sold. An overly intrusive government, or large bureaucracy is often the cause of corruption and malfeasance.

For example, two recent stories in the news today reports drug lord Joaquin "El Chapo" Guzman paid a 100 million dollar bribe to former Mexican President Enrique Peña Nieto in 2012, and then there is the Mayor of New York City, Bill de Blasio, whose new plan is for the city's government to seize buildings of landlords who don't run their buildings according to their arbitrary rules.

These are just minor examples of government corruption and overreach by powerful GBs, and they are the tip of the iceberg. The larger the government, the greater the corruption. Smaller governments always, always have less power to encourage corruption. When government controls strongly influence business practices, corporations have far more incentive to try to buy that government influence.

Limited government means just that: fewer rules. Money and resources that would otherwise be devoted to complying with overzealous regulations can be used for more productive purposes. More individual freedom and the right to do what you want, as long as you don't infringe on anyone else's rights, will become the norm under the *Gamacode*.

Adam Smith said it best in his Book the Wealth of Nations published March 9, 1776. It is as relevant today as it was over 250 years ago, and the reason is simple: Human nature does not change. He called it the "Invisible Hand."

Limited government favors few, if any, controls, not only on a nation's individuals but on its economy. Let supply-and-demand forces – Smith's "Invisible Hand" theory – drive the economy and do not allow the GB to intervene, to alter, or influence economic cycles and business activity.

Thus, the *Gamacode* will be limited in size proportional to the number of the beings it represents. A small GB will insure the power remains with the beings of the planet. Clever officials will try to increase their workforce with the excuse there are not enough staff to adequately serve the citizens. This is fallacy. A well-run GB operation will have more than enough resources to accomplish whatever needs its citizens require. Gone are the days when department heads must spend their allotted budgets or suffer cutbacks the following fiscal period. Gone are the days when budgets are increased automatically with little or no regard for performance. Efficiency, responsibility, and frugality of the workforce will be rewarded for their conscientious service to the community, not punished.

Contribution: Investopedia.com: REVIEWED BY Will Kenton  Updated Mar 28, 2018

As a lobbyist, I was completely against term limits, and I know a lot of people are against term limits, and I was one of the leaders, because why? As a lobbyist, once you buy a congressional office, you don't have to re-buy that office in six years, right?

Jack Abramoff

Too many in Washington display a ruling class mentality, and congressional term limits would go a long way towards restoring the citizen-legislator ethos of the Founding Fathers.

Ron DeSantis

Term limits aren't enough. We need jail.

P. J. O'Rourke

We are just fools. We insanely believe that we can replace one politician with another and something will really change. The ONLY possible way to achieve change is to change the very system of how government functions. Until we are prepared to do that, suck it up for your future belongs to the madness and corruption of politicians.

Anon

# Rule Twelve

"A Governing Body official or representative cannot serve more than one, three-year term in their lifetime.

In general, politicians are self-serving. It really does not matter which party we are discussing. The problem with politics has been that the people have been so complacent, that the politicians feel as if they can do anything with total immunity. The Clintons set up a Canadian branch for their charity so that they would not have to disclose their donors, but it is now known there were 1,100 undisclosed donors to the Clinton Foundation, all of a foreign origin. Dick Cheney's old company, Halliburton, moved to Dubai for the same reason. And let us not forget Hillary amazing commodity trading ability back in 1994 when she made over 180,000 dollars on a single trade!

House Minority Leader Nancy Pelosi saw her net worth rise 62 percent last year, cementing her status as one of the wealthiest members of Congress. This amazing, almost no-loss, increase in wealth by members of Congress and political elite, can be seen on both sides of the aisle. It is a given, the longer one stays in office, the larger one's assets will increase in valve. This, of course, does not include the generous pensions public servants receive after retirement. Senator Diane Feinstein draws a $53,068 pension from the city and county of San Francisco, where she served 18 years as mayor and as a member of the Board of Supervisors, along with her 175,000 Senators salary.

So why do politics attract people who want to get rich quick? The only way to force honesty is with term limits. We can't afford career politicians any longer. Especially lawyers, for they are trained in knowing how to circumvent the law legally. Government should reflect the people – not a single profession. We need laws that prohibit someone from being the head of anything, such as the IMF, unless they have experience in the financial markets.

Elected officials quickly forget why they were sent to represent the beings who voted for them. In early days of the Republic, representatives would serve one or two terms, earn 6 dollars a day while Congress was in session, and then go home to resume their lives they had before going to Washington. That is not so today. Lucrative salary packages, generous benefits, free health care, free travel, and full pensions after serving one term have turned once thoughtful legislators into career politicians. Their excuse has been we are doing the work of the people; because we are experience in the ways of government, we are the only ones best suited for the job. This mentality is now common and so has led to abuse and corruption of their office. Allowing only one term over a lifetime for any publicly elected official, no matter how good and honest they appear to be, will eliminate this career practice. Nor will a public servant be allowed to serve one term as President and a second term as Vice President, a third term as Secretary of State, and on and on. One 3-year term, and one term only in any public office, will be the strict limit for any individual. Let the act of public representation be a noble one rather a place of enrichment. Add to that, no GB official will collect a pension when their service has completed. True public servants will require only a small annual salary or stipend for their work, and then like all good public servants, resume the lives they had before becoming an elected GB official.

Contributor: Armstrong Economics Blog: May 5, 2015 by Martin Armstrong

(1) Public service is a public trust, requiring employees to place loyalty to the Constitution, the laws and ethical principles above private gain.(2) Employees shall not hold financial interests that conflict with the conscientious performance of duty.  Code of Federal Regulations (CFR) Section 2635.101

# Rule Thirteen

"A Governing Bodies cannot have rights; they
have a duty to the beings they represent and the
Gamacode."

According to the Code of Federal Regulations (CFR) Section 2635.101 Basic obligation of public service, subsection (a) Public service is a public trust. Each employee has a responsibility to the United States Government and its citizens to place loyalty to the Constitution, laws and ethical principles above private gain.

This regulation sounds wonderful on its surface. Public servants are hired or elected to ensure that the public's money is spent as efficiently as possible and that programs are provided effectively, without discrimination or prejudice, with transparency and without waste of money or resources. But as we all know, there are those that will try to abuse this public trust. The problem arises when this trust is broken; there are rarely any consequences for inappropriate behavior. The elite hierarchy of the GB through their various associates, partners in crime, back room deals and unspoken alliances, you scratch my back, I'll scratch yours, etc. are rarely made to account for their mishandling of the public trust.

This practice will end in all forms with the *Gamacode*.

Because there is a greater trust that goes with representing the public, those public servants whether elected or not have a "special duty" and a higher responsibility to those they serve. Although the public servant has equal rights as everyone else in the community, they are subject to an even greater obligation to the public they represent. The *Gamacode* does not recognize government self-imposed laws that protect the incompetent, negligent, or corrupt public servant. If those public servants are found guilty of abuse and corruption, they will suffer double the punishment or, in the most immoral, corrupt, and abusive cases will be exiled to the Tinkerville off-world facility, or equal, with no possibility of return.

"I could end the deficit in five minutes. You just pass a law that says that anytime there is a deficit of more than 3% of GDP all sitting members of congress are ineligible for reelection."

Warren Buffet

# Rule Fourteen

## "GBs are subject to the laws they pass."

So often the ruling class of GBs create and pass laws that are never intended for them. For example, the U.S. Congress is allowed to pass legislation that pertains only to itself or which pertains to all but the Congress. A classic example is that Congress originally exempted itself from Social Security taxes, meaning that members of Congress did not have to pay into the Social Security Trust Fund.

Another example of Congressional exemption is the Freedom of Information Act. The public can request information from federal agencies, but Congress, the federal courts and some parts of the Executive Office of the President are exempt.

If asked whether a GB representative must comply with the laws it passes, one would answer yes, of course. But many representatives would be against that. As stated above, elected officials today often pass laws that except themselves, and they have done so repeatedly.

In ancient Sparta the same laws of the city-state applied even to the kings.

The *Gamacode* will change this practice and return the Spartan justice back to GBs.

GBs will live under the same roof as everyone else. No one or no group will be above the law. No special privileges are given to any representative or their staff. Any law, regulation, or mandate passed by the GB will affect everyone equally, including the GB, judges, and its workforce, no exception.

A grand jury could "indict a ham sandwich," if that's what you wanted because the prosecutors are totally unsupervised in bringing indictments. Thomas Wolf, *Bonfire of the Vanities*

# Rule Fifteen

## "A GB cannot have the power to prosecute."

Prosecution without responsibility is not justice. GBs get to use an endless supply of public tax money to obstruct lawsuits and obstruct the gathering of evidence. A citizen suing any GB needs more than just a winning case, they need an incredible amount of resources.

"For example, when it came time to print our brief to submit to the U.S. Court of Appeals, I figured I could have printed it at home for about a $20 cost in terms of ink and paper. I could have had it printed at a professional printing center for about $40.

"But in our legal system, those aren't options. The procedures require us to have the brief professionally printed and bound in a book format. And only certain companies may be used for this service.

"So how much was it to print the briefing in the required format?

"Instead of $20, it was $4,367.70. Just to print a brief.

"As for attorney's fees, my appellate attorney was kind enough to offer a deep discount, and his law students generously donated some of their time. But the cost of the work just for the appeal alone — a few months of the four years of legal work to date —

totaled over $100,000.

"You can see how justice quickly becomes cost-prohibitive and simply out of reach."

Sharyl Attkisson: "A Citizen Suing the Dept. of Justice needs more than just a Winning Legal Argument". *American Thinker,* Feb. 21, 2019

Because GB prosecutions have few or no penalties for senseless lawsuits and tribunals, aggressive GB prosecutors have little incentive to protect the innocent. Successful trials, not justice for the accused who can be threatened with years of jail time, can be abusive. The U.S. Justice Department claims discretion to obey the law. This is why elite politicians can escape prosecution because the government can deny equal protection of the law to its citizens. They prosecute some people and not others for the very same offense. We must always remember to protect the majority from the ruthless, abusive power of the minority.

Martin Armstrong makes a strong point: "We seriously MUST take away the power to prosecute from the government. Any crime should be limited to VIOLENCE that results in prison and ALL prosecutions MUST be at the signed request of a citizen. If the citizen files a false charge, then they should suffer the same fate that they sought against the individual. We simply have to end political prosecutions. That power MUST be stripped from governments when we get to reset the entire system once they crash and burn as a result of their own corruption."

Ordinary citizens do not have the millions of dollars it takes to pursue justice against an adversary that has unlimited time and money. They have to give up. The *Gamacode* will put an end to this abusive practice of GBs to prosecute.

He who is being carried does not realize how far the town is.
Nigerian Proverb Rule

# Rule Sixteen

## "A GB cannot create a Welfare State."

The welfare state is where the GB provides, promotes, and subsidizes the social and economic well-being of its citizens. It is based on the principles of "equality of opportunity, equitable distribution of wealth, and public responsibility for those unable to avail themselves of the minimal provisions for a good life." GB social programs of all types, whether they be for "the Children," the poor, or some other deprived group, it is mandated that everyone must pitch in to help those in need. This is a big mistake. Regardless of one's political ideals, taking money from one person to give to another makes no sense. If a private person, group, or business wishes to subsidize or fund a charity for the poor, the children, abused spouses, or whatever the cause, that is an entirely different matter. It's their money. They can spend it however they want. As long a no GB is involved or forcing anyone to pay for a particular group the *Gamacode* is not violated.

One must keep in mind that since President Johnson began the War on Poverty back in 1964, despite $12 trillion in federal welfare spending and $3 trillion in state and local government welfare spending over the past 50 plus years, the poverty rate has never fallen below 10.5 percent, and today it is at its highest level in nearly a decade, 15.1 percent and climbing. Clearly, the welfare states globally are a failure and a waste of time and money.

So why do we continue to throw good money after bad? The answer is quite simple: Most of the money goes for government services and administration through its salaried posts and government funded agencies. Interestingly, less than 5% of government spending is spent on reducing inequality and poverty. Most of the tax dollars is spent on employing people who provide the services. In other words, the greatest beneficiaries of the Welfare State are the people who are fortunate enough to be employed directly, or indirectly, by these government or GB controlled agencies.

But, but "we benefit the poor," they say. Yet these employed GB employees enjoy very high salaries, comfortable lifestyles, all funded by the tax payer. It is almost as if, when we work for government people don't see themselves as beneficiaries, instead they see themselves entitled to such high salaries, pensions, and power because 'the poor' are lucky to be getting their services for doing God's work. This self-righteousness is on a grand scale and it encourages a deeply patronizing attitude to those who live in poverty.

The danger of the welfare state, is that it sucks the lifeblood of our freedom and resources from the community to fund this boondoggle. The GB becomes all too powerful, unyielding, cumbersome, and a disempowering system that doesn't even tackle the most basic problem - poverty. The money raised in taxes does not go to those in need, it goes to the better off. In other words, it goes to the GB that justifies its existence by the 'good' it appears to do.

The *Gamacode* would eliminate GB run welfare state forever!

"Blessed are the Children, for they shall inherent the National Debt."

Quote taken from a fortune cookie.


"To preserve our independence, we must not let our rulers load us with perpetual debt. We must make our election between economy and liberty, or profusion and servitude."

Thomas Jefferson

# Rule Seventeen

## "A GB cannot issue debt or operate in a deficit."

There will be many who would argue that a panic in government debt markets would never happen. In fact, this is the precise thing that has ALWAYS happened whenever government debt has grown to an alarming level in history.

The Truth About The Great Depression:

While many economists would like you to believe that the Great Depression was all about greed and speculation, the truth of the matter is that it was about a massive worldwide default in government debt! All of Europe permanently defaulted on its debt with the exception of a six month moratorium in Britain. All of South and Central America permanently defaulted as well as most of Asia. The German bond default of 1931 involved $12 billion alone and it took the BIS (Bank of International Settlements) until 1937 to calculate the total debt that was permanently wiped out. This stands in stark contrast to the peak in broker loans on the NYSE in 1929 which had stood at only $6.5 billion.

"The Constitution simply does not authorize the federal government to own any of this land. All of it is being held unconstitutionally and all of it should be returned to the private property owners from which it was taken or to the states in which it exists, period."

Judge Andrew Napolitano

# Rule Eighteen

## "A GB cannot own land."

It is generally believed that a GB exists to serve the public good. Owning or taking land using funds collected from community can lead to corruption, often taking the best land for the GB's own use. Let's look at the percentage of Federal ownership of land in just three states: Nevada, 81 percent. Utah, 66 percent. Idaho, 61 percent. So one must ask why the government owns any land?

Under the Property Clause (Art. IV, Sec. 3, Cl. 2), land titled to the federal government and held outside state boundaries is "Territory." Federal land held within state boundaries is "other Property."

So the debate's short answer is that the Constitution, through the Property Clause, specifically gives the government the power to own land. Over time, the Supreme Court has ruled that not only does the government own the land, but it enjoys broad rights in deciding what happens on that land.

In 2007, the Congressional Research Service, the nonpartisan research arm that works on behalf of Democrats and Republicans, explored the legal roots of federal land ownership. Its finding was unambiguous.

"The Property Clause gives Congress authority over federal

property generally, and the Supreme Court has described Congress' power to legislate under this Clause as 'without limitation'," the researcher wrote.

The Heritage Foundation, a conservative think-tank and activist organization in Washington, D.C., says much the same thing on its online guide to the Constitution. It provides the key text from Article IV of the Constitution. "The Congress shall have Power to dispose of and make all needful Rules and Regulations respecting the Territory or other Property belonging to the United States."

Columbia Law School professor Thomas Merrill, noted that many people have debated the scope of this clause. The most narrow interpretation, Merrill wrote, "simply allows Congress to act as an ordinary owner of land. It can set policy regarding whether such lands will be sold or retained and, if they are retained, who may enter these lands and for what purposes."

The *Gamacode* will end this back and forth debate. The abuse of such power is too great. A GB cannot own land other than to rent or lease for necessary purposes allowed by the community. It shall not be dictating how land is used in any community or enforcing its will over the authority of local elected officials.

"Every gun that is made, every warship launched, every rocket fired signifies in the final sense, a theft from those who hunger and are not fed, those who are cold and are not clothed. This world in arms is not spending money alone. It is spending the sweat of its laborers, the genius of its scientists, the hopes of its children. This is not a way of life at all in any true sense. Under the clouds of war, it is humanity hanging on a cross of iron."

Dwight D. Eisenhower

It is forbidden to kill; therefore all murderers are punished unless they kill in large numbers and to the sound of trumpets.

Voltaire

War HAS NEVER changed anything. NEVER! Everything continues as it always has. You lie to yourself if you believe it has changed anything. History always repeats itself because human beings refuse to learn.

Anon

# Rule Nineteen

### "A GB cannot create a secret, clandestine organization or military force."

America has been at war continuously for over 15 years. With the help of a willing mainstream media, no one seems to notice, but men and women all over the world are fighting, dying and returning wounded every day, and the great majority of this people are young people. Military forces and secret bodies within the GB have no place in a free and open society. These armed forces are often turned against the very citizens they were created to protect. Wars are caused, not by the citizens of the community, but by GBs and bankers who fund them, in order to control the population. Without a military force to back them up, the plotters of war have no means to accomplish their goals of domination over other beings in society. There will always be bullies in every society who wish to control others, but if the means of control is forbidden, well-armed citizens can protect themselves. Peaceful coexistence between societies can and will prevail. Given the choice of slavery or freedom, beings will always choose freedom.

# Rule Twenty

"A GB cannot revoke the Gamacode."

There are those over time who will try to alter the rules of the *Gamacode* like they have with the U.S. Constitution. They will fail! They will say it is just a document of words. That it is a "living document" that can be changed according to the times. They will try to tweak it here and there to allow the GB to expand and return to its oppressive nature. Small changes at first, but like the camel putting his nose in the tent, they will try to find a way to change what cannot be changed. There is nothing to add or subtract from the *Gamacode*. It is irrevocable and will not be amended, changed, or modified. The CODE IS LAW and will always be the law of the planet and the universe, for if we are to survive as species, we must remove the shackles that got us here. Those shackles have ALWAYS been the Kings, Queens and Governing Bodies that have ALWAYS stifled the beings they rule over from becoming the best they can be. We must strive for freedom. No Governing Body has ever granted beings their liberty, their self-determination, their personal sovereignty willingly. We must take it and keep it once it is obtained. The *Gamacode* is the absolute and unequivocal path to freedom. The *Gamacode* does not require trust or acceptance. No

Governing Body is exempt. The *Gamacode* is not living, transitional, or temporary. The *Gamacode* is enduring and forever. Governing Bodies and/or individuals violating the *Gamacode* will be immediately exiled to an off-world facility with no recourse of return and that will be the way of the planet and the Universe to the end of time...

# Rule Twenty-one

"What the Gamacode does not cover is left to the GB of the particular society, country, or state they represent, to run as they choose, as long as there is no violation of the Gamacode."

It is the belief of the Gamadin that free beings everywhere are willing and able to govern themselves. Free and open societies grow, prosper, and live in harmony with each other when left to their own choices. There is no Utopia. Beings living together will always have conflict. Murder, theft, fraud, and the destruction of other being's property will not cease. But it will be up to the local community to solve those problems, not an all-knowing, faceless GB. This is not to say that beings living in free societies have the right to do anything they wish. As stated previously, the *Gamacode* rules protect the public against the overreaching power of a central Governing Body. The local laws of the community remain intact as long as the *Gamacode* itself is not violated. At all times the GB must respect the fundamental rights of the individual to live a free and prosperous life of one's own choosing. If a being wishes to live in filth, that is their choice, but a being that has criminal intent, is destructive of other beings' rights and property, will not be tolerated and should be dealt with swiftly and punished as the community sees fit. The *Gamacode* does not interfere with a community's laws unless the *Gamacode* is violated.

"GBs are like little puppies. They start out all warm and fuzzy when they are small, but then they grow into monsters. Even Godzilla was a baby once."

Tom Kirkbride, author Gamadin Book Series

# Taming Godzilla

Now that the rules have been set for the Governing Bodies of the planet, how will the structure of the *Gamacode* be implemented? What non-human mechanism will insure the rules of the Code are carried out planet-wide?

To answer this most important question of all we turn to the American *Declaration of Independence*. After it was signed there needed to be a structure or framework for the new country to follow. The Colonies first attempt was the *Articles of Confederation*. It was argued that it lacked enforcement powers to carry out its rules. However, the colonies became paralyzed, and the Articles failed but not for the reason often stated. The *Articles of Confederation* was a wonderful structure. The reason it failed was not from weakness, but because it was too strong. The powers that be were too restricted. It would not allow the expansion of human involvement. Human nature's desire to control the beings of the community overpowered the intent of the *Articles of Confederation*, tying the hands of those in authority. In short, it stunted baby Godzilla's growth. It was believed that to be effective a more powerful central government with enforceable powers was necessary to replace the weaker *Articles of Confederation*. From this failure, the *U.S. Constitution* was born. And as we are very aware today, the granddaddy of all Godzillas has become a reality.

As stated many times, history shows us that all forms of governing bodies, no manner how well constructed to maintain the freedom and liberty of the beings under it, ultimately fail because human nature never changes. A being's desire to control other beings ultimately takes over, and we begin the whole cycle over again. The Baby Godzilla grows up syndrome is repeated turning a once free population into slaves of the GB once again.

To solve this problem and to keep Godzilla from becoming an adult but remaining a juvenile, better yet staying a baby, the planet must have a central authority of its own, free of human intervention to guard against its growth. An all-powerful god-like approach is one solution. An example of this can be found in the 1951 American movie: *The Day the Earth Stood Still.* In the story, an alien visitor, Klaatu, addresses the world and tells Earth's inhabitants he is a representative of an interplanetary organization that created a police force of invincible androids like the nine-foot robot, Gort. "In matters of aggression," Klaatu states, "we have given them (Gort) absolute power over us." Klaatu concludes, "Your choice is simple: join us and live in peace, or pursue your present course and face obliteration."

Turning control over to an all-powerful robot or A.I. would be extremely frightening to most beings. The what-if possibilities are endless. What if the robot's software is hacked, or if the A.I. is taken over by a tyrant? Then what? The entire planet could be subject to mass slavery.

Another solution, however, and one that does not require an all-powerful robot or god-like central intelligence is called the "blockchain." By design, a blockchain is decentralized, unalterable, and incorruptible. It is "an open ledger of record transactions between two parties that is verifiable in a permanent way. Once recorded, the data in any given block cannot be altered without all subsequent blocks agreeing to the network majority. It is the ultimate, decentralized authority and will become the heart of a planet-wide compliancy.

How would the *Gamacode* work inside this blockchain?

Take any rule, like Rule #11: "A Governing Body and its

workforce and representatives cannot be greater than one, one thousandth percent (.001) of the population." If a GB were to expand beyond the one, one thousandth percent size of its workforce and representatives, the blockchain would automatically trip the enforcement mechanism, which in this case, might be to shut down all power to that particular GB until the blockchain has affirmed Rule #11 is back in compliance. This could go even go farther if this was a serious offense by the GB representatives who wanted to control more of the beings they serve. In such a case, those representatives found guilty, the blockchain would then call for the excommunication of those representatives. Power would only be restored when the blockchain had been satisfied.

Plug any *Gamacode* rule into the above scenario and the answer will be the same. The *Gamacode* must be in compliance and affirmed by the blockchain at all times or power to the GB will be cut. Any GB that tries to circumvent the power restriction will be subject to an even greater consequence, such as mass arrests and excommunications of its representative workforce until such time the blockchain is satisfied and the Rule is in agreement.

Finally, each community will be responsible to maintain their own GB's compliance. It is not a community's business what another GB does. The blockchain is the overseer. This linkage of the Gamacode to a planet-wide blockchain will guarantee in perpetuity that the freedom and liberty is never lost and that the GB is never allowed to grow into a monstrous Godzilla again!

SO LET FANTASY BE REALITY...

AND LET THIS CODE BE THE BEGINNING
OF OUR TRUE FREEDOM AS A PLANET!

# Final Quotes on Freedom

"One of the saddest lessons of history is this: If we've been bamboozled long enough, we tend to reject any evidence of the bamboozle. We're no longer interested in finding out the truth. The bamboozle has captured us. It's simply too painful to acknowledge, even to ourselves, that we've been taken. Once you give a charlatan power over you, you almost never get it back."

Carl Sagan, *The Demon-Haunted World: Science as a Candle in the Dark*

"I am for doing good to the poor, but...I think the best way of doing good to the poor, is not making them easy in poverty, but leading or driving them out of it. I observed...that the more public provisions were made for the poor, the less they provided for themselves, and of course became poorer. And, on the contrary, the less was done for them, the more they did for themselves, and became richer."

Benjamin Franklin

Government is actually the worst failure of civilized man. There has never been a really good one, and even those that are most tolerable are arbitrary, cruel, grasping, and unintelligent.

H. L. Mencken

Unfortunately the Federal Government has strayed far afield from its legitimate business. It has trespassed upon fields where there should be no trespass. If we could confine our Federal expenditures to the legitimate obligations and functions of the Federal Government, a material reduction would be apparent. But far more important than this would be its effect upon the fabric of our constitutional form of government, which tends to be gradually weakened and undermined by this encroachment.

Calvin Coolidge

"Is life so dear, or peace so sweet, as to be purchased at the price of chains and slavery? Forbid it, Almighty God! I know not what course others may take, but as for me, give me liberty or give me death!"

Patrick Henry

All difficult things have their origin in that which is easy, and great things in that which is small.

Taoist Proverb

09202019a

www.ingramcontent.com/pod-product-compliance
Lightning Source LLC
Chambersburg PA
CBHW021849170526
45157CB00007B/3013